POWER HABIT MORNING ROUTINE:

The 30 Minute Quick Guide for Busy People

The 7 Steps You Can Take Now That Will Transform Your Fitness, Increase Your Knowledge and Improve Your Productivity Each Day

ROMNEY NELSON

POWER HABIT MORNING ROUTINE

© COPYRIGHT 2020 THE LIFE GRADUATE PUBLISHING GROUP
ALL RIGHTS RESERVED.

The content contained within this book may not be reproduced, duplicated or transmitted without direct written permission from the author or the publisher.

Under no circumstances will any blame or legal responsibility be held against the publisher, or author, for any damages, reparation, or monetary loss due to the information contained within this book. Either directly or indirectly.

Legal Notice:

This book is copyright protected. This book is only for personal use. You cannot amend, distribute, sell, use, quote or paraphrase any part, or the content within this book, without the consent of the author or publisher.

Disclaimer Notice:

Please note the information contained within this document is for educational and entertainment purposes only. All effort has been executed to present accurate, up to date, and reliable, complete information. No warranties of any kind are declared or implied. Readers acknowledge that the author is not engaging in the rendering of legal, financial, medical or professional advice. The content within this book has been derived from various sources. Please consult a licensed professional before attempting any techniques outlined in this book.

By reading this document, the reader agrees that under no circumstances is the author responsible for any losses, direct or indirect, which are incurred as a result of the use of the information contained within this document, including, but not limited to, — errors, omissions, or inaccuracies.

POWER HABIT MORNING ROUTINE

-Take Action Daily-
Life is too short to hesitate!

TABLE OF CONTENTS

INTRODUCTION	1
WHAT ARE GOOD HABITS AND BAD HABITS?	12
BEFORE WE COMMENCE WITH THE 7 STEPS	15
THE 7 STEPS TO DEVELOP A GREAT MORNING HABIT ROUTINE	19

- STEP 1 – GOALS CREATE OUR 'WHY'
- STEP 2 – INCREMENTAL CHANGE PLAN
- STEP 3 – MAKE IT EASY
- STEP 4 - REPETITION
- STEP 5 – LAYERING HABITS
- STEP 6 – STRUCTURE YOUR MORNING
- STEP 7 – CONSISTENCY IS KEY

GETTING YOU STARTED	35

- MAKE IT PERSONAL TO YOU

QUICK GUIDE SUMMARY	38

- BECOME COMMITTED AND TAKE ACTION

THE 30 MINUTE QUICK GUIDE SERIES	41

- DEVELOP THE PLAN TO ACHIEVE YOUR GOALS

ABOUT THE AUTHOR	43

POWER HABIT MORNING ROUTINE

INTRODUCTION

Changing your daily habits is a powerful tool, but it can be challenging to know where to start. When figuring out which habits you should prioritize to improve your health, wealth and knowledge, it is helpful to have an example of a good set of habits. I want to provide you with my personal list of habits before we commence this quick guide that I do every day to ensure I am making progress towards my goals. My clients have made significant progress since having access to this structure. This guide will provide you with a template to base your morning habits off and help you define what you want to achieve and the way you want to achieve it.

Scheduling your habits throughout the day can be the difference between diligently keeping them and letting them fall by the wayside. Think about what you want to accomplish each day. These should be small scale changes and activities that you can repeat and turn into habits over time. Then arrange these actions into a schedule that fits with your needs and your lifestyle, creating patterns and routines you stick to nearly every day.

Routines in the morning are essential, so focus on these, to begin with. Morning routines help you wake up refreshed and ready to succeed over all of the day's challenges. They help you achieve more, think clearly, and do work that matters. Structuring your day around habits and routines that support your health, fitness, knowledge and productivity will help you get closer to your goals each day.

Everyone's habits are going to be different; your daily morning habits should be reflective of what you value, what you want to improve, and the time you can commit to each goal you have. By sharing my habits, I hope to guide you through the process I used to select my own habits and show how they each support my endeavors.

My personal mantra is "What can I do today that will further my personal growth and move me closer to reaching my full potential tomorrow?" Every day should bring you closer to reaching your potential. As you will find out as you read this quick guide, I don't advocate for perfectionism, but rather personal fulfilment. You should strive to become the best possible version of yourself, not someone else. This means following your own dreams, not the goals someone else has set for you. As a result, I develop my habits based on my personal goals because they are made up of the things that I want for myself and my family. This includes my physical health as well as my mental well-being. Our bodies are the vehicles we need to achieve all of our goals, so we owe it to ourselves to look after the gift and opportunity we have been given.

How I Established My Habit Schedule

My habit schedule is influenced by who I am as a person. People who know me well appreciate that I am well-structured, organized and very focused. I also consider myself to be committed to the goals I set for myself. As a result, I schedule my habits with the aim to do them at the same time every day. Having a schedule to fall back on reinforces positive behaviors and helps me keep track of my progress. Because of this, I have scheduled my habits in a way that allows me to maximize their benefits and give them an appropriate amount of time. I make sure to avoid rushing a new or developing habit so that it "takes root" firmly and develops correctly. I try to focus on each individually and give them time to develop incrementally so that I don't overwhelm myself.

My diet is one area that I pay careful attention to. A healthy, nutritious diet provides me with the energy I need to accomplish all of my other goals, so I need to ensure I am keeping myself in the best possible shape. I would consider my diet to be well balanced, mainly as a result of my upbringing, my background in sports, and my qualifications in physical education and health. I always want to embody what I suggest for others. If I encourage others to eat certain foods and maintain a balanced diet or to exercise a certain way, it's because I do it myself. Of course, I also think it is important to highlight that I do still drift on occasions from a diet of nutritious foods. I still have the occasional pizza, a beer with family and friends, a good coffee, and even a great muffin. These little treats can be nice to enjoy now and then. However, I try to keep them to a minimum in my diet. My personal eating habits restrict less healthy foods to around five percent of my overall diet. This leaves plenty of room for more nutritious options most days, which bring me closer to my goals of living a long and healthy life. I fill the rest of my diet with healthy foods that provide my body with the fuel I need to take me to my 100th birthday.

Exercise is another important part of my morning habit routine. It is a habit that I picked up when I was younger while training for competitive sports, however, I recognize that this is not true for everyone and that as we age, exercise becomes about finding sustainable activities we can integrate into our lives without increasing the chance of injury. Many friends of mine who have sustained injuries during competitive sports and long-distance running do have limitations with their mobility. When finding the right exercise for you, it is critical to take into account your limitations and choose something you can do regularly.

Ultimately, my morning habits are structured to provide long-term support and assistance on my journey to reach my goals, which is the same idea you should take into account when deciding on your own morning habits. I will expand on the methods I use to narrow down the habits that best suit my lifestyle, as well as how I began implementing these habits and building them incrementally so they can build up to compounding effects over time. However, I want to provide a word of warning first. The habits that work well for me may not be suitable for you. I am using my personal schedule in the book primarily to illustrate the power of morning habits and what they allow you to do, not to suggest you copy my habits directly. They are suited to my own long-term goals, but they may not be reflective of yours. Spend some time thinking about what you want to achieve and how you would be able to go about achieving it as you create your list of daily supportive habits.

My Morning Routine

I have outlined below my morning routine, which I hope serves as an introduction and a template for your own. Use it to get an idea of my structure and how I have been able to incorporate ten healthy and supportive habits over 2 hours that cover my fitness, knowledge and productivity.

5:00 AM - Wake up

5:35 AM - Power walk with my dog and listen to an educational podcast

5:15 AM - Drink 500 mL water and take one magnesium supplement

5:20 AM - Breakfast of porridge with fresh fruit and one scoop of natural yoghurt

5:30 AM - 120 push-ups (4 sets of 30)

5:40 AM - 200 sit-ups (4 sets of 50)

5:50 AM - Personal daily goal affirmations (recorded and played back)

5:55 AM - Meditation and visualization for 15 minutes

6:15 AM - The Daily Goal Tracker: record what I'm grateful for, my current thoughts, and my 3 TOP Priority Actions for work for that day.

6:35 AM - Shower

6:50 AM - Reading for 30+ minutes

7:30 AM - Begin the day

These habits are short activities that take up a small portion of my day. They are not too difficult for me to complete, which means I have no trouble repeating them each morning. Over the course of one month, assuming I do these habits six days a week and use Sunday as my rest and recovery day, they build up to a powerful transformation.

Here is the massive compounding impact I receive by the end of the month:
- Walking/exercise = **12 hours**
- Podcasts (inspirational interviews) = **12 hours**
- Push-ups = **2,880** push-ups for upper body strength and tone
- Sit-ups = **4,800** sit-ups for core strength and avoiding lower back pain.
- Planting my goals subconsciously via daily affirmations = **2 hours**
- Meditation/visualization = **12 hours**
- Prioritization of daily activities to move closer to my goals = **72 key actions**
- Journaling six things I am grateful for daily = **24 days of journaling**
- Reading = **12 hours**

You can now see just how much of an impact mini habits can have on your life. If I simply decided to do 4,800 sit-ups in a month without any other planning, I would likely end up slacking some days and failing to reach my goal. By breaking the process up into more bite-sized, easily achievable sections each day, I have no trouble reaching my goal. I hope that you can use this process of establishing mini habits to achieve the same levels of tremendous change and amazing results for your health, diet, energy levels, knowledge and productivity.

What are Good and Bad Habits?

What differentiates a good habit from a bad one? Simply put, a good habit is anything that helps you in building a better version of yourself. Good habits help you unlock your potential and meet your goals. They may help you improve your knowledge and education, your fitness, your physical or mental health, your wealth, or any number of other positive goals. They may also make you happier, but in the more fulfilled sense that comes from completed goals and realized aspirations rather than the fleeting sort of happiness that comes from a single leisure activity.

Bad habits, on the other hand, are habits that stand in the way of your goals. They are detrimental to your growth and only restrict you from all you could otherwise achieve. Bad habits are often time wasters like television binges and oversleeping. Social media is another common time sink that can prevent productivity. They are also activities with negative impacts on your health, such as overeating, lack of exercise, smoking, and excessive drinking. If a habit isn't helping you to achieve your goals, then it is hurting you, and you should take the necessary steps to replace it as soon as possible. Though you may give up the initial small bursts of false happiness that come with eating junk food or watching your third basketball game in a row, you will exchange them for something much more real and concrete with a notable impact on your life.

Before we commence with the 7 Steps

It is an essential stage of this quick guide to breaking down the process of how to put a new morning habit into action, and this is by introducing it incrementally. To provide you with a clear example, let us assume that you currently rise at 7:00 AM, but you would like to get up at 6:20 AM so that you can add in an extra 30 minutes of reading in your day. Merely setting the alarm for 6:20 AM and trying to change your schedule with no build-up preparation is likely to get you hitting the snooze button, which could lead to you accidentally sleeping in even later than your usual time. If you take the time to wake up five minutes earlier every few days incrementally, something that takes much less willpower will easily allow you to reach 6:20 AM with minimal effort or impact on your alertness or energy levels.

I have used this example to great effect in my book 'Magnetic Goals'. In the example I offer the following strategy;

Start by initially setting your alarm five minutes earlier every third day, six days per week, with Sunday being a day when you can sleep in. The schedule shows how a small change every three days would play out, allowing you five minutes to get out of bed and perhaps make a cup of tea before beginning to read.

Week 1,
Mon/Tues/Weds: 6:55 AM alarm, no reading at this stage.

Week 1
Thurs/Fri/Sat: Alarm is wound back by 5 minutes to 6:50 AM. Still no reading at this stage.

Week 2
Mon/Tues/Weds: 6:45 AM alarm, 10 minutes of reading commences

Week 2
Thurs/Fri/Sat: Alarm is brought back to 6:40 AM alarm, permitting 15 minutes of reading

Week 3
Mon/Tues/Weds: 6:35 AM alarm, 20 minutes of reading

Week 3
Thurs/Fri/Sat: Alarm is brought back to 6:30 AM alarm, permitting 25 minutes of reading

Week 4
Mon/Tues/Weds: 6:25 AM alarm, 30 minutes of reading

Week 4,
Thurs/Fri/Sat: Alarm is brought back to

6:20 AM alarm, permitting you to reach you goal of 35 minutes of reading

In just 30 days, you have shifted your schedule to achieve a 6:20 AM start to your day, and you have accumulated over two hours of reading in the process. This is great, but the biggest change will now start to compound, now that you have extra time in your schedule to read.

Over one year, you will have an extra 40 minutes in your schedule, six days a week, 52 weeks a year, totalling an extra 208hrs in your schedule. This is the equivalent of adding 8 ½ additional days to your year. If you can keep this up for five years, you can achieve 1,032 extra hours or 43 days you did not have access to before. Trust me; you won't miss the 40 minutes of sleep each day in the face of the significant benefits you will receive. Being able to read hundreds of books you would have otherwise missed out on can produce amazing, substantial changes in your life and improve your skills and knowledge.

The 7 Steps to Develop a Great Morning Habit Routine

Step 1 – Goals Create our 'WHY'

The starting point for Habit Development is to establish your goals. Your goals will provide the core focus and direction for your morning habit routine, and become your WHY?

To develop good daily habits, you need to understand what motivates you and why it does so. An equally strong and supportive reason for each strong and supportive habit will ensure that you keep doing the habit for as long as necessary. If you understand why something is important and why you want to get it done, you will spend less time fighting with yourself and simply buckle down and do it.

Everything you are doing should matter in one way or another. Whether you enjoy the task itself or you are simply pursuing the outcome, you should understand the reasons behind your actions. There are so many distractions that make it easy to fill our lives up with things that don't really matter to us. The trick is to ask ourselves how we spend less time doing unimportant things and more time doing the things we love to do. Always question what your 'why factor' is for each new activity or habit that enters your life.

ACTION STEP

To begin, write down what your goals are that you will achieve from your morning routine. Is it to exercise more, read more, gain greater productivity from the day? By writing down your goals, we can then establish our habit change plan and incrementally build it for long-term success.

Step 2 – Incremental Change Plan

A critical part of developing your morning routine is the development of your initial habit plan. Your plan provides the structure so you can incrementally build on your habits to allow the compounding impact to play its part.

The ultimate plan is to start with small changes, and that paves the way for much larger ones. Without the development of strong and consistent daily habits, you will be unable to commit yourself to the daily habits that allow you to achieve success, but this does not mean pushing yourself out of your comfort zone right away. Never expect to adopt a habit immediately, especially when it makes a big impact.

An Example of how I established a supportive habit

Introduction of Supportive Habit #1:
Writing down my top three priorities and key actions for the following day.

Reason:
Introducing this habit would allow me to have clarity and focus on my most important tasks for the next day. I could go to bed confident in the progress I will make tomorrow, and I will allow my subconscious to arrange the next day while I sleep. I then have confidence that I can wake up ready to tackle my most important tasks.

Incremental Change:
I started by setting the alarm at 5:30 PM. Even if I hadn't finished my other work by then, I stopped and grabbed my notepad to write down just my number one priority for the next day. I did this for three days, after which I reviewed and increased this to two priorities

for seven days. Again, I reviewed and then increased to three key tasks. I always listed my number one priority at the top and used tick boxes to mark my progress to build confidence.

Long-term Results:
From just this one successfully implemented habit, I found that I had much more clarity going into the next day. I was more relaxed at night, and my focus was crystal clear.

To understand the benefits of starting small when building up strong habits, let's look at another example. Say you are not a swimmer, but you want to train for a .6-mile (1 km) swim. If you started trying to swim .6 miles every day with no prior training, you would exhaust yourself every time and likely become discouraged due to a lack of progress. If instead, you began at two laps and added just one more lap to your practice each day, you could comfortably push your limits without completely burning yourself out. Swimming only one extra lap is not an especially hard task, which makes it easy to add to your routine. An extra lap is around 25 m, so it would take you roughly 10 -12 weeks to build up to your ultimate goal. This may take a bit longer than short term, intense training sessions, but it forms the basis for continued practice and improvement while also minimizing the chance that you simply give up halfway through or suffer an overuse injury. That would ultimately be the worst possible outcome and could delay your progress for months. You can apply this strategy of incremental improvement to any habit or goal.

Another Practical Application –
Example of introducing an earlier wake-up time and daily reading. The ultimate being a 5.30 AM wake-up and 30 minutes reading.
Your priority is to introduce the change in small increments:
Application:
Stagger your alarm times to be set 10 minutes

earlier each week for 8 weeks. That way, you will not even notice the difference. Remember, don't rush the change as this is a 'long-term' commitment, so 8 weeks in the grand scale of the change is very insignificant. Introduce just 5 minutes of reading each morning for Week 1. Increase the reading by 5 minutes each week for 6 weeks = 30 minutes.

Step 3 – Make it Easy.

When implementing habits, some may be more difficult than others. Make them as easy as possible to adopt by creating the lowest resistance to starting. Keep your habits small until you know you can do them. You may want to arrange things the night prior to starting a habit, so you have fewer reasons not to do it the next day. It also means having a specific time set for exercise. The structure will aid you immensely.

My personal example for my morning walks:
- Before going to bed each night, I get my exercise gear ready. This way, I'm not fumbling around in the dark to get what I need.
- I pre-set my podcast so I can just hit play.
- The dog leash is ready at the back door.

By getting all of this done the night before, getting ready to exercise only involves getting out of bed and getting dressed.

Step 4 – Repetition

Generally, habits take about 60 to 90 days of implementation to be fully integrated into your brain. This can vary depending on the *'frequency'* of the activity, but more often than not, you will need to perform a habit for an extended period before it becomes an unconscious process. Repetition is key. This is also true of unlearning bad habits. Unfortunately, it takes as long to unlearn a bad habit as it does to learn a good one, but you can train yourself out of any habits that might be holding you back with enough time and dedication. Save yourself the time by avoiding developing bad habits in the first place and doing things the right way the first time rather than taking shortcuts or losing focus.

Step 5 – Layering Habits

You don't want to overwhelm yourself with too many new habits at once. Some people attempt to change many parts of their lives at once and end up overburdening themselves with expectations that they are unable to meet all at the same time. They end up jumping from one thing to another in rapid succession and never really feel comfortable with any individual habit. If these new habits are simply spread out over a longer period of time; however, you can be much more successful at adopting them. If you are trying to start five new habits, it is more sensible to introduce one new habit each week. By the time five weeks are up, you will have five new habits that all fit comfortably into your existing schedule. By layering your new habits in this manner, you can determine which ones work and which ones do not. You can also make adjustments to how long you spend on each habit. If you try to include 30 minutes of informative reading into your schedule each day, but find that it intrudes too much upon your other responsibilities, you can easily identify the need to cut reading time down to 20 minutes rather than trying to sort through five different habits to find the problem. Keep making adjustments over the course of a week until you find the schedule that fits your lifestyle best.

Step 6 – Structure Your Morning

You are more likely to stick to habits if they become part of your daily structure. An excellent way to guarantee this is to write your habits down as part of your schedule. Writing your habits down helps you to maintain accountability for completing them each day and keep them present in your mind as you work the habit into your daily life over a couple of months. List your habits like a to-do list, including the actions you need to complete as well as the times you should start and finish them. Keeping your habits organized in a to-do list is a great way to give your daily activities structure and ensure you complete everything you need to do each day.

Structuring your daily habits is an extremely important step for establishing a robust system. After a few weeks, you will start developing a dependency on completing them and become addicted to the amazing results they will help you achieve. The stronger your structure, the greater the chance that your habits will become ingrained into your routine and become automatic.

Step 7 – Consistency is Key.

Momentum and change build confidence. We need to view our progress as motivational and let it carry us through to future successes. When you really care about what you are doing, every step you take will feel like its own success. These simple, one percent changes that you make every day or even every week can exponentially improve your self-esteem, especially when you learn to recognize their huge compounding impact.

Ongoing improvements always make a difference, no matter if it is just one percent. That doesn't seem like a lot on its own, but just like habits, it can build up into something amazing. You only need to be willing to commit yourself to make tiny improvements regularly. To become one percent better each day, you need to focus on your reasons for self-improvement, the personal gratification you feel when you improve, maintaining a long-term view, and ensuring you take action consistently.

Don't miss more than two consecutive days
Taking long breaks between your habits can cause them to fade out of your body's memory. Staying consistent is especially important during the early phases of building a habit, as taking breaks longer than 48 hours can start to weaken the links that turn habits into an automatic process. If you need to rest, it is better to take two non-consecutive days off.

Getting You Started.

1. **Write down your goals** – This will enable you to develop your habit plan
2. **Become committed to change** – Are you ready for change, and are you ready to fight back against distraction and your old habits creeping back?
3. **Start with just one** – Begin with just one very small habit change and start to implement it slowly for the next 7 days. Remember, by building slow; you will develop a long-term supportive habit that could be with you forever.

Habits that I have that you may like to incorporate into your AM Routine.
- *30 Mins Exercise*
- *Drink 500 mL water + one magnesium supplement*
- *Healthy Breakfast*
- *Push-ups for strength and tone*
- *Sit-Ups for core body strength and tone*
- *Daily Goal Affirmations*
- *Meditation/Visualization*
- *Gratitude Journaling*

POWER HABIT MORNING ROUTINE

- *Listing my TOP 3 Priority Actions for work for that day.*
- *Reading*

Quick Guide Summary

- Engaging in the right daily habits establishes a sturdy structure to build future successes
- Good habits help you improve yourself and get closer to your goals, while bad habits impede your progress
- Set new supportive habits and rid yourself of all of your bad habits through repetition of positive actions
- Figure out why you want to achieve your goals to give you the motivation to start new habits and get ahead of the competition
- Start small and build up to big changes
- Introduce new habits one at a time, and keep a tight schedule of your daily habits
- Exercise to provide yourself with a focus boost and shake off sleep
- Eating a healthy breakfast provides you

with plenty of energy to get your day moving
- Visualize your goals each morning to help your subconscious mind
- Dedicate time to self-improvement by reading or listening to audiobooks and podcasts
- List the goals you need to get done at the start of every day

My Free GIFT for You

To get you started, I have created a Morning Habit template that you can print off, plug in your times and get ready to start your '**Power**' Morning.

Visit the following link to download it.

https://thelifegraduate8265.activehosted.com/f/17

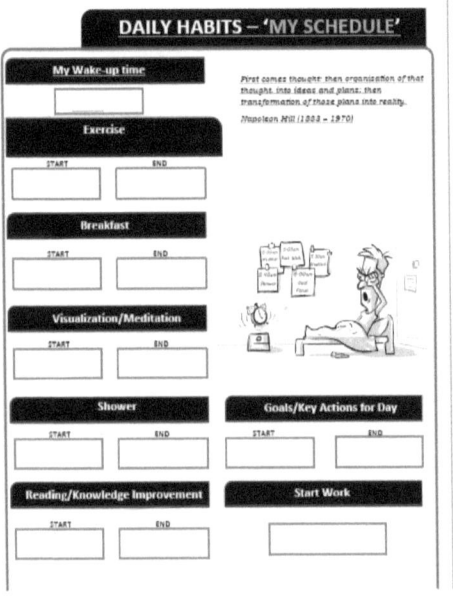

The 30 Minute 'Quick Guide' Series

Available through all major online bookstores in eBook and paperback format.

NOW available in Audiobook!

PLEASE LEAVE A REVIEW

Thank you for reading the 30-minute guide. My aim is to provide great information that will help as many people as possible. The way you can help and to positively impact others is by leaving a review, thus, in turn, spreading the word so others can improve their lives. I read every review I get, and it helps me to make improvements and also know if you love my books.

About the Author

Romney is an Amazon Best Selling Author and the founder of The Life Graduate Publishing Group.

He represented Australia in the World Championships in 1988 in Dragon Boat Racing; he is a business coach, motivational speaker, qualified teacher, author and owner of two rapidly growing businesses in the educational space.

Romney has dedicated the past 20 years to helping others achieve success and fulfilment in their lives through his coaching, teaching, masterclasses, mentoring, resources and books. His clients speak of his passion and dedication for self-improvement and bringing that knowledge and experience to help others achieve what they want in their lives.

Romney is a sought-after speaker and is regarded as one of the leading experts in goal setting and daily habits with the development of the unique Dr ACTION™ and 'The Goal Loop' systems. He has a Bachelor of Education in Physical Education, is a qualified Personal Trainer and has previously held Head of Faculty positions in some of the most prestigious schools in Australia. He has also held senior executive positions in leading start-up companies.

Additional Books

www.ingramcontent.com/pod-product-compliance
Lightning Source LLC
LaVergne TN
LVHW090039080526
838202LV00046B/3888